Prai ther

Christian or 7s to 14s

A companion volume to Sing to God
compiled by Margaret V. Old

Scripture Union
130 City Road, London EC1V 2NJ

First published 1984

ISBN 0 86201 206 6

Printed in Great Britain at The Pitman Press, Bath

CONTENTS

WE PRAISE GOD

1. *The Father, Son and Holy Spirit*

1

Don Fishel

Chorus:
Alleluia, alleluia, give thanks to the risen Lord!
Alleluia, alleluia, give praise to his name.

1. Jesus is Lord of all the earth.
He is the king of creation.
Chorus:

2. Spread the good news through all the earth,
Jesus has died and has risen.
Chorus:

3. We have been crucified with Christ –
now we shall live for ever.
Chorus:

4. God has proclaimed the just reward –
life for all men, alleluia!
Chorus:

5. Come, let us praise the living God,
joyfully sing to our Saviour!
Chorus:

2

Dale Garratt

Alleluia! for the Lord our God the almighty reigns;
alleluia! for the Lord our God the almighty reigns:
let us rejoice and be glad and give the glory unto him:
alleluia! for the Lord our God the almighty reigns.

3

Hazel Hudson

1. Christ is with the Father now,
praise to you, praise to you!
Let us praise and thank him now,
glory, Lord, to you!
Alleluia, let us sing,
praise to you, praise to you!
Glory to our heav'nly king,
glory, Lord, to you!

2. Let us sing and let us play,
praise to you, praise to you!
Praises let us sing today,
glory, Lord, to you!
Alleluia, let us sing,
praise to you, praise to you!
Glory to our heav'nly king,
glory, Lord, to you!

4

Unknown

1. Come into his presence singing,
'Alleluia, alleluia, alleluia!'*

2. Come into his presence singing,
'Jesus is Lord, Jesus is Lord, Jesus is Lord!'

3. Come into his presence singing,
'Worthy the Lamb, worthy the Lamb, worthy the Lamb!'

4. Come into his presence singing,
'Glory to God, glory to God, glory to God!'

* *Each verse should be sung twice*

5

Bob McGee

Emmanuel, Emmanuel,
his name is called Emmanuel.
God with us, revealed in us,
his name is called Emmanuel.

6

Donna Adkins

1. Father, we love you,
we worship and adore you.
Glorify your name in all the earth.
Glorify your name,
glorify your name,
glorify your name in all the earth.

2. Jesus, we love you,
we worship and adore you.
Glorify your name in all the earth.
Glorify your name,
glorify your name,
glorify your name in all the earth.

3. Spirit, we love you,
we worship and adore you.
Glorify your name in all the earth.
Glorify your name,
glorify your name,
glorify your name in all the earth.

7

from Gloria in Excelsis
Christopher Idle

1. Glory in the highest to the God of heaven!
Peace to all your people through the earth be given!
Mighty God and Father, thanks and praise we bring,
singing alleluia to our heavenly king.

2. Jesus Christ is risen, God the Father's Son!
With the Holy Spirit, you are Lord alone!
Lamb once killed for sinners, all our guilt to bear,
show us now your mercy, now receive our prayer.

3. Christ, the world's true Saviour, high and holy one,
seated now and reigning from your Father's throne:
Lord and God, we praise you! Highest heaven adores:
in the Father's glory, all the praise be yours!

8

A Rische

1. God is all-loving; he has redeemed me,
God is all-loving, and he loves me.
Chorus: *And so I sing again, God is all-loving,*
God is all-loving, and he loves me.

2. Your love is patient with my shortcomings.
Your love upholds me in all my need.
Chorus:

3. O love eternal, I'll ever praise you.
For evermore your love I'll proclaim.
Chorus:

9

Unknown

Hallelu, hallelu, hallelu, hallelujah;
we'll praise the Lord! } twice
We'll praise the Lord, hallelujah!
We'll praise the Lord, hallelujah!
We'll praise the Lord, hallelujah!
We'll praise the Lord!

10

Alex Simons and Freda Kimney

God is our Father,
for he has made us his own,
made Jesus our brother,
and hand in hand we grow together as one.

Sing praise to the Lord with tambourine.
Sing praise to the Lord with clapping hands.
Sing praise to the Lord with dancing feet.
Sing praise to the Lord with our voice,
la la la la la la
la la la la la la la
la la la la la la
la la la la la la la la la la la

11

Unknown

His name is higher than any other,
his name is Jesus, his name is Lord;
his name is higher than any other,
his name is Jesus, his name is Lord.
His name is Wonderful, his name is Counsellor,
his name is Prince of Peace, the mighty God;
his name is higher than any other,
his name is Jesus, his name is Lord.

12

Audrey Mieir

His name is wonderful,
his name is wonderful,
his name is wonderful,
Jesus my Lord;
he is the mighty king,
master of everything,
his name is wonderful,
Jesus my Lord.
He's the great shepherd,
the rock of all ages,
almighty God is he;
bow down before him,
love and adore him,
his name is wonderful,
Jesus my Lord!

13

Unknown

1. Holy, holy, holy is the Lord;
holy is the Lord God almighty!
Holy, holy, holy is the Lord;
holy is the Lord God almighty,
who was, and is, and is to come:
holy, holy, holy is the Lord!

2. Jesus, Jesus, Jesus is the Lord;
Jesus is the Lord God almighty . . .

3. Worthy, worthy, worthy is the Lord;
worthy is the Lord God almighty . . .

4. Glory, glory, glory to the Lord;
glory to the Lord God almighty . . .

14

Mary Lathbury
adapted by Margaret Old

Holy, holy, holy, Lord God of hosts!
Greater than all things that live,
hear the praises that we give,
O Lord most high!

15

Joseph Hart

1. How good is the God we adore,
our faithful unchangeable friend!
His love is as great as his power,
and knows neither measure nor end!

2. 'Tis Jesus the first and the last,
whose Spirit shall guide us safe home;
we'll praise him for all that is past,
we'll trust him for all that's to come.

16

Unknown

How great is our God! How great is his name!
How great is his love, for ever the same!
He rolled back the waters of the mighty Red Sea,
and he said, 'I'll never leave you; put your trust in me.'

17

Unknown

In the name of Jesus, in the name of Jesus
we have the victory;
in the name of Jesus, in the name of Jesus,
Satan will have to flee.
Who can tell what God can do?
Who can tell of his love for you?
In the name of Jesus, Jesus,
we have the victory.

18

David Mansell

1. Jesus is Lord! Creation's voice proclaims it,
for by his power each tree and flower
was planned and made.
Jesus is Lord! The universe declares it –
sun, moon and stars in heaven cry: 'Jesus is
Lord!'

Chorus: *Jesus is Lord, Jesus is Lord!*
Praise him with alleluias,
for Jesus is Lord!

2. Jesus is Lord! Yet from his throne eternal
in flesh he came to die in pain on Calvary's tree.
Jesus is Lord! From him all life proceeding –
yet gave his life a ransom thus setting us free.

Chorus:

3. Jesus is Lord! O'er sin the mighty conqueror;
from death he rose and all his foes
shall own his name.
Jesus is Lord! God sends his Holy Spirit
to show by works of power that Jesus is Lord.

Chorus:

19

Lenny Smith

How lovely on the mountains are the feet of
him
who brings good news, good news!
Announcing peace, proclaiming news of
happiness:
our God reigns, our God reigns,
our God reigns, our God reigns,
our God reigns, our God reigns.

20

Unknown

I will enter his gates with thanksgiving in my
heart,
I will enter his courts with praise;
I will say this is the day that the Lord has made,
I will rejoice for he has made me glad.
He has made me glad, he has made me glad,
I will rejoice for he has made me glad.
He has made me glad, he has made me glad,
I will rejoice for he has made me glad.

21

Edna Bird

Chorus: *Join with us to sing God's praises,*
for his love and for his care,
for the happiness he gives us,
praise him for the world we share.

1. Thank him for the town and country,
thank him for the sun and rain,
thank him for our homes and gardens,
sing his praises once again.

Chorus:

2. We have eyes to look around us,
we have strength to work and play,
we have voices we can use – to
sing his praises every day.
Chorus:

3. Praise him in your words of kindness,
praise him helping those in need,
praise him in your thought for others,
sing his praises with each deed.

22

Richard Bewes

1. Let us sing to the God of salvation,
let us sing to the Lord our rock!
Let us come to his house with thanksgiving,
let us come before the Lord and sing!

Chorus: *Praise our maker, praise our Saviour,*
praise the Lord our everlasting king.
Every throne must bow before him,
God is Lord of everything!

2. In his hands are the earth's deepest places
and the strength of the hills is his!
All the sea is the Lord's, for he made it,
by his hand the solid rock was formed.
Chorus:

3. Let us worship the Lord our maker,
let us kneel to the Lord our God;
for we all are the sheep of his pasture,
he will guide us by his powerful hand.
Chorus:

4. Let today be the time when you hear him!
May our hearts not be hard or cold,
lest we stray from the Lord in rebellion,
as his people did in time of old.
Chorus:

23

Unknown

My God[1] is so great,
so strong[2] and so mighty[3]
there's[4] nothing my God cannot do.
My God[1] is so great,
so strong[2] and so mighty[3]
there's[4] nothing my God cannot do.
The mountains[5] are his,
the rivers[6] are his,
the stars[7] are his handiwork, too.
My God[1] is so great,
so strong[2] and so mighty[3]
there's[4] nothing my God cannot do.

Actions

1. *Slowly stretch arms up and out*
2. *Raise right clenched fist*
3. *Raise left clenched fist*
4. *Stretch arms wide*
5. *Form mountain with finger tips*
6. *Move hands left to right fluttering fingers*
7. *Point to several stars in sky*

24

Joanne Pond

O give thanks to the Lord, all you his people,
O give thanks to the Lord for he is good.
Let us praise, let us thank, let us celebrate and
dance.
O give thanks to the Lord for he is good.

25

Norman Warren (Psalm 149)

Chorus: *O praise the Lord, O praise the Lord,*
sing to the Lord a new song;
O praise the Lord, O praise the Lord,
sing out his praises all people of God!

1. Let us praise him in the dance,
let us praise him on the strings,
let us all be joyful in our king:
Chorus:

2. Victory belongs to him,
justice, mercy, truth are his,
for the Lord takes pleasure in his people:
Chorus:

26

Derek Haylock

Praise God in his holiness;
praise him in his awesome power;
praise him for his mighty deeds;
let us praise him every hour!
Praise him for his sovereign strength;
praise him for his faithfulness;
all creatures in earth and heav'n,
praise his love and righteousness.

Hallelujah! Trumpets, sound!
Cymbals, drums and strings, abound!
Words alone cannot be found to praise him,
hallelujah!
To God we our worship bring,
adore him for everything;
and this psalm of praise we sing;
hallelujah! Praise God!

27

Unknown
Jubilate Hymns version

1. Praise him, praise him,
everybody praise him –
he is love, he is love;
praise him, praise him,
everybody praise him –
God is love, God is love!

2. Thank him, thank him,
everybody thank him –
he is love, he is love;
thank him, thank him,
everybody thank him –
God is love, God is love!

3. Love him, love him,
everybody love him –
he is love, he is love;
love him, love him,
everybody love him –
God is love, God is love!

4. Alleluia,
glory, alleluia!
He is love, he is love;
alleluia,
glory, allelulia!
God is love, God is love!

28

Peter Casey

1. Praise the Lord in the rhythm of your music,
praise the Lord in the freedom of your dance,
praise the Lord in the country and the city,
praise him in the living of your life!

2. Praise the Lord on the organ and piano,
praise the Lord on guitar and on the drums,
praise the Lord on the tambourine and
cymbals,
praise him in the singing of your song!

3. Praise the Lord with the movement of your
bodies,
praise the Lord with the clapping of your
hands,
praise the Lord with your poetry and painting,
praise him in the acting of your play!

4. Praise the Lord in the feeding of the hungry,
praise the Lord in the healing of disease,
praise the Lord as you show his love in action,
praise him in your caring for the poor!

5. Praise the Lord, every nation, every people,
praise the Lord, men and women, old and
young,
praise the Lord, let us celebrate together,
praise him everything in heaven and earth!

29

Thomas Ken
Jubilate Hymns version

Praise God from whom all blessings flow,
in heaven above and earth below;
one God, three persons, we adore –
to him be praise for evermore!

30

Norman Warren and Margaret Old

1. Praise the Lord, praise the Lord my soul!
I'll praise the Lord as long as I live.
Chorus: *And I will sing a song, sing a song,*
sing a song to him,
a song of praise to my God all my life.

2. The Lord who died – he's alive for evermore.
The Lord who died – he is with us today.
Chorus:

3. The Lord is king, he is king for evermore;
the Lord is king, he will reign for all time.
Chorus:

31

Unknown

1. Sing praises to God, sing praises,
sing praises to God, sing praises,
for he is the king of all the earth,
sing praises to his name.

2. Give honour to God . . .

3. Give glory to God . . .

32

Estelle White

Praise to the Lord our God, let us sing together,
lifting our hearts and our voices to sing with
joy and gladness.
Come along, along, along and sing with . . . .
(repeat)

4-part round

33

from Psalm 98
Michael Baughen

1. Sing to God new songs of worship –
all his deeds are marvellous;
he has brought salvation to us
with his hand and holy arm:
he has shown to all the nations
righteousness and saving power;
he recalled his truth and mercy
to his people Israel.

2. Sing to God new songs of worship –
earth has seen his victory;
let the lands of earth be joyful
praising him with thankfulness:
sound upon the harp his praises,
play to him with melody;
let the trumpets sound his triumph,
show your joy to God the king!

3. Sing to God new songs of worship –
let the sea now make a noise;
all on earth and in the waters
sound your praises to the Lord:
let the hills be joyful together,
let the rivers clap their hands,
for with righteousness and justice
he will come to judge the earth.

34

Unknown

1. Sing to the Lord a joyful song,
for he has done great things,
and he has won the victory:
and he has won the victory.
Rejoice and praise the Lord!
Rejoice and praise the Lord!
Rejoice, rejoice, and praise the Lord!

2. Sing to the Lord a glad new song,
he's made salvation known,
and he has shown his righteousness:
and he has shown his righteousness.
So let all nations sing! (twice)
So let, so let all nations sing!

3. Sing to the Lord a joyful song,
his faithful love endures,
and to the world he shows his grace:
and to the world he shows his grace.
Rejoice and praise the Lord! (twice)
Rejoice, rejoice, and praise the Lord!

4. Sing to the Lord a glad new song,
with music praise his name:
let everyone sing praises;
let everyone sing praises.
So let all nations sing! (twice)
So let, so let all nations sing!

5. Sing to the Lord a joyful song;
he comes to rule the earth,
with righteousness and truth:
with righteousness and truth.
Rejoice and praise the Lord! (twice)
Rejoice, rejoice, and praise the Lord!

6. Glory to God the Father be,
and glory to the Son,
and glory to the Spirit be:
and glory to the Spirit be.
Both now and evermore,
both now and evermore;
Amen, Amen, Amen, Amen!

35

Unknown

Wherever I am I'll praise him,
whenever I can I'll praise him;
for his love surrounds me like a sea.
I'll praise the name of Jesus,
lift up the name of Jesus,
for the name of Jesus lifted me.

36

Estelle White

With a song in our hearts we shall go on our way,
to bring God's love to ev'ryone we meet today.
Love, love, love is his name.
Love, love, love is his name.
Great, great, great is his name.
Great, great, great is his name.
With a song in our hearts we shall go on our way,
to bring God's love to ev'ryone we meet today.

37

Mavis Ford

You are the King of glory, you are the Prince of peace,
you are the Lord of heaven and earth,
you're the sun of righteousness!
Angels bow down before you, worship and adore,
for you have the words of eternal life,
you are Jesus Christ the Lord!
Hosanna to the Son of David, hosanna to the King of Kings!
Glory in the highest heaven for Jesus the Messiah reigns!

2. *He made us and cares for us*

38

Michael Cockett

Chorus: *All the nations of the earth,*
praise the Lord who brings to birth
the greatest star, the smallest flower.
Alleluia.

1. Let the heavens praise the Lord.
Alleluia!
Moon and stars, praise the Lord.
Alleluia!
Chorus:

2. Snow-capped mountains, praise the Lord.
Alleluia!
Rolling hills, praise the Lord.
Alleluia!
Chorus:

3. Deep sea water, praise the Lord.
Alleluia!
Gentle rain, praise the Lord.
Alleluia!
Chorus:

4. Roaring lion, praise the Lord.
Alleluia!
Singing birds, praise the Lord.
Alleluia!
Chorus:

5. Kings and princes, praise the Lord.
Alleluia!
Young and old, praise the Lord.
Alleluia!
Chorus:

39

Estelle White

1. Autumn days when the grass is jewelled,
and the silk inside a chestnut shell,
jet planes meeting in the air to be refuelled,
all these things I love so well.
Chorus: *So I mustn't forget,*
no, I mustn't forget,
to say a great big thank you.
I mustn't forget.

2. Clouds that look like familiar faces,
and a winter's moon with frosted rings,
smell of bacon as I fasten up my laces,
and the song the milkman sings.
Chorus:

3. Whipped-up spray that is rainbow-scattered,
and a swallow curving in the sky.
Shoes so comfy though they're worn-out and
they're battered,
and the taste of apple-pie.

Chorus:

4. Scent of gardens when the rain's been falling,
and a minnow darting down a stream,
picked-up engine that's been stuttering and
stalling,
and a win for my home team.

Chorus:

40

Caroline Somerville

1. God Almighty set a rainbow
arching in the sky above,
and his people understand it
as a signal of his love.

Chorus: *Thank you, Father, thank you, Father,*
thank you, Father, for your care,
for your warm and loving kindness
to your children everywhere.

2. Clouds will gather, storms come streaming
on the darkened earth below –
too much sunshine makes a desert,
without rain, no seed can grow.

Chorus:

3. Through the stormcloud shines your rainbow,
through the dark earth springs the wheat.
In the future waits your harvest
and the food for men to eat.
Chorus:

4. God Almighty, you have promised
after rain the sun will show;
bless the seeds and bless the harvest.
Give us grace to help us grow.
Chorus:

41

Fred Pratt Green

1. God in his love for us lent us this planet,
gave it a purpose in time and in space:
small as a spark from the fire of creation,
cradle of life and the home of our race.

2. Thanks be to God for its bounty and beauty,
life that sustains us in body and mind:
plenty for all, if we learn how to share it,
riches undreamed of to fathom and find.

3. Long have the wars of man ruined its harvest;
long has earth bowed to the terror of force;
long have we wasted what others have need of,
poisoned the fountain of life at its source.

4. Earth is the Lord's: it is ours to enjoy it,
ours, as his stewards, to farm and defend.
From its pollution, misuse and destruction,
good Lord deliver us, world without end!

42

Peggy Blakeley

1. Give to us eyes
that we may truly see
flight of a bird,
the shapes in a tree,
curve of a hillside,
colours in a stone.
Give to us seeing eyes, O Lord.

2. Give to us ears
that we may truly hear
music in birdsong,
rippling water clear,
whine of the winter wind,
laughter of a friend.
Give to us hearing ears, O Lord.

3. Give to us hands
that we may truly know
patterns in tree bark,
crispness of the snow,
smooth feel of velvet,
shapes in a shell.
Give to us knowing hands, O Lord.

43

Archie Hall

He made the stars to shine,
he made the rolling sea,
he made the mountains high,
and he made me.
But this is why I love him,
for me he bled and died,
the Lord of all creation,
became the crucified.

44

Alex Mitchell

1. Now we sing a harvest song,
clear and joyful, loud and strong;
think of bread and think of meat,
think of all we have to eat;
all God's gifts to us in love,
earth and rain and sun above,
thank you, God, for all you give,
thank you, God, by whom we live.

2. Now we sing a sadder song
of injustice, hunger, wrong;
those with not enough to eat,
scarcely bread, and never meat;
have no home, no work, no pay,
scraping through from day to day.
Do they thank you that they live?
Thank you, God, that we can give.

3. As we sing our harvest song,
clear and joyful, loud and strong,
help us, Father, now to see
how to set those people free;
how to share the gifts you give
so that they may also live,
so the harvest song may sound
to your praise the earth around.

45

M V Old

1. O Lord our great God, how majestic your name is!
How great is your name, Lord, in all the wide earth!
Your glory is higher than all your creation,
and children sing praises that tell of your worth.

2. I think of the worlds that you've hung out in space, Lord,
the moon and the stars – all creation above,
and wonder how ever you think of each person
and want us, each one, to discover your love.

3. Yet man is unlike all earth's creatures, for in the
beginning God made us his image to bear.
He crowned man with glory and honour, and told us
that we in his work of dominion might share.

46

Rosamond Herklots

1. Our God is one who makes things.
All life in earth or star
is there because he wakes things
and makes them what they are.
So often we mistake things
and mix up bad and good,
and then we spoil and break things
and feel misunderstood.

2. We all can learn to make things
if that is what we want,
perhaps to sew or bake things,
perhaps to build or plant.
It's easier to break things,
but when we've once begun
with hands and minds to make things,
it's hard but much more fun.

3. God's Spirit works to shake things
until at last we see
how sadly we mistake things,
how different life could be.
We need not spoil or break things,
let's build and not destroy.
We'll work with God to make things
and share our maker's joy.

47

Brian Wren

1. Praise God for the harvest of farm and of field,
praise God for the people who gather their
yield,
the long hours of labour, the skills of a team,
the patience of science, the power of machine.

2. Praise God for the harvest that's sent from afar,
from market and harbour, from tropical shore:
foods packed and transported, and planted and
grown
by God-given neighbours, unseen and
unknown.

3. Praise God for the harvest that comes from the
ground,
by drill or by mineshaft, by opencast mound;
for oil and for iron, for tinplate and coal,
praise God, who in love has provided them all.

4. Praise God for the harvest of science and skill,
the urge to discover, create and fulfil:
for all new inventions that promise to gain
a future more hopeful, a world more humane.

5. Praise God for the harvest of conflict and love,
for leaders and peoples who struggle and serve
to conquer oppression, earth's plenty increase,
and gather God's harvest of justice and peace.

48

Doreen Newport

1. Think of a world without any flowers,
think of a world without any trees,
think of a sky without any sunshine,
think of the air without any breeze.
We thank you, Lord, for flow'rs and trees and sunshine,
we thank you, Lord, and praise your holy name.

2. Think of a world without any animals,
think of a field without any herd,
think of a stream without any fishes,
think of a dawn without any bird.
We thank you, Lord, for all your living creatures,
we thank you, Lord, and praise your holy name.

3. Think of a world without any people,
think of a street with no one living there,
think of a town without any houses,
no one to love and nobody to care.
We thank you, Lord, for families and friendships,
we thank you, Lord, and praise your holy name.

49

Paul Booth

1. Who put the colours in the rainbow?
Who put the salt into the sea?
Who put the cold into the snowflake?
Who made you and me?
Who put the hump upon the camel?
Who put the neck on the giraffe?
Who put the tail upon the monkey?
Who made hyenas laugh?
Who made whales and snails and quails?
Who made hogs and dogs and frogs?
Who made bats and rats and cats?
Who made ev'rything?

2. Who put the gold into the sunshine?
Who put the sparkle in the stars?
Who put the silver in the moonlight?
Who made Earth and Mars?
Who put the scent into the roses?
Who taught the honey bee to dance?
Who put the tree inside the acorn?
It surely can't be chance!
Who made seas and leaves and trees?
Who made snow and winds that blow?
Who made streams and rivers flow?
God made all of these!

50

Robin E Littler

Venus, Mercury, Pluto, Mars,
'twas God who made them all.
Blazing sunshine, twinkling stars,
'twas God who made them all.
The planets and all things in space,
the world and men of ev'ry race,
were all created by his grace,
Jesus, wonderful friend.

51

Gracie King, altd.

1. When I see the salmon leap the fall,
or the aer'plane's silver trail –
or a drop of water magnified,
then my eyes and heart bless the Lord.

2. When I hear the frosty crunch of snow,
or the sun-drenched hum of the bee,
or a well-tuned engine whine with power,
then my ears and heart bless the Lord.

3. When I breathe the smell of clean fresh air
blowing softly after rain,
when the strawberries are turned to jam,
then my nose and heart bless the Lord.

4. At the taste of berries gathered free,
or the tang of sea-food, mint or treacle,
touch of velvet, feel of cold smooth stones,
hands and tongue and heart bless the Lord.

JESUS CHRIST

1. When Jesus was born

52 *Timothy Dudley-Smith*

1. A song was heard at Christmas
to wake the midnight sky:
a Saviour's birth, and peace on earth,
and praise to God on high.
The angels sang at Christmas
with all the hosts above,
and still we sing the newborn king,
his glory and his love.

2. A star was seen at Christmas,
a herald and a sign,
that men might know the way to go
to find the child divine.
The wise men watched at Christmas
in some far eastern land,
and still the wise in starry skies
discern their maker's hand.

3. A tree was grown at Christmas,
a sapling green and young:
no tinsel bright with candlelight
upon its branches hung.
But he who came at Christmas
our sins and sorrow bore,
and still we name his tree of shame
our life for evermore.

4. A child was born at Christmas
when Christmas first began:
the Lord of all a baby small,
for love of men made man.
For love is ours at Christmas,
and life and light restored,
and so we praise through endless days
the Saviour, Christ the Lord.

53

Traditional

This carol is sung progressively. A song leader sings the first line, others respond, 'How will you send me?', and the song leader replies, for the first verse, 'Oh, I will send you one by one . . .' etc. The second time the song leader responds with, 'Oh, I will send you two by two,' and the others join in. Here is the last verse.

Leader: Children, go, I will send you.

All: How will you send me?

Leader: Oh, I will send you six by six –
six for the stars that shone in the sky,

All: five for the snow that lay on the ground,
four for the oxen that stood in the stall,
three for the good old wise men,
two for Joseph and Mary,
one for the little bitty baby boy, boy
born in Bethlehem, Bethlehem,
Bethlehem.

54

Geoffrey Ainger

1. Born in the night,
   Mary's child,
   a long way from your home;
   coming in need,
   Mary's child,
   born in a borrowed room.

2. Clear shining light,
   Mary's child,
   your face lights up our way;
   light of the world,
   Mary's child,
   dawn on our darkened day.

3. Truth of our life,
   Mary's child,
   you tell us God is good;
   prove it is true,
   Mary's child,
   go to your cross of wood.

4. Hope of the world,
   Mary's child,
   you're coming soon to reign;
   King of the earth,
   Mary's child,
   walk in our streets again.

55

Malcolm Sargent

1. Girls and boys, leave your toys, make no noise,
kneel at his crib and worship him.
At thy shrine, child divine, we are thine,
our Saviour's here.

Chorus: *'Hallelujah' the church bells ring,*
'Hallelujah' the angels sing,
'Hallelujah' from everything.
All must draw near.

2. On that day, far away, Jesus lay,
angels were watching round his head.
Holy child, mother mild, undefiled,
we sing thy praise.

Chorus:

3. Shepherds came at the fame of thy name,
angels their guide to Bethlehem.
In that place, saw thy face filled with grace,
stood at thy door.

Chorus:

56

Michael Perry

1. Happy Christmas, everybody!
All the world is singing;
come to worship, everybody,
praise and glory bringing.

Chorus:
Come into his church with praise,
come in through those doors to thank him.

2. Happy Christmas, everybody!
Join his people praying;
God is speaking, everybody,
hear what he is saying.

Chorus:

3. Happy Christmas, everybody!
God's new day is dawning;
meet the Saviour, everybody,
Christ is born this morning.

Chorus:

Happy Christmas, everybody,
Christ is born this morning!

57

Valerie Collison

1. Have you any room (keep knocking)?
Have you any room at all?
Is anybody there,
does anybody care?
Have you any room at all?

2. Have you any room, (keep knocking)?
Have you any room at all?
I've just a cattle shed,
a manger for a bed,
but you're welcome to the stall.

3. Just a manger bare for Jesus,
just a lowly cattle stall,
but angels in the sky
are praising God on high.
Christ is born, the Lord of all!

4. Have you any room for Jesus?
Have you any room at all?
He longs to be your friend,
his love will never end.
Have you any room at all?
Have you any room at all?

58

Richard Avery and Donald Marsh

Chorus: *Hey! Hey! Anybody listening?*
Hey! Hey! Anybody there?
Hey! Hey! Anybody listening?
Anybody care?

1. We've got good news, good news, good news, good news:
Christ the Lord will soon be found here!
Good news, good news, good news, good news:
let's help spread the news around here!
If I had a drum I'd drum it,
a mandolin I'd strum it,
a humming bird hum I'd hum it,
everywhere, everywhere, everywhere, everywhere.
Chorus:

2. People come on, come on, come on, come on:
let's sing out for Mary's son here!
Come on, come on, come on, come on:
he'll bring joy for everyone here!
If I had a harp I'd twang it,
a tambourine I'd bang it,
a fireman's bell I'd clang it,
everywhere, everywhere, everywhere, everywhere.
Chorus:

3. Come on, sing out, sing out, sing out, sing out!
Tell the world about his birth now!
Sing out, sing out, sing out, sing out
loud and clear to all the earth now!
If I had a chime I'd ring it,
a finger cymbal ching it,
we've got this song let's sing it,
everywhere, everywhere, everywhere,
everywhere.

59

Timothy Dudley-Smith

1. Holy child, how still you lie;
safe the manger, soft the hay,
faint upon the eastern sky
breaks the dawn of Christmas Day.

2. Holy child, whose birthday brings
shepherds from their field and fold,
angel choirs and eastern kings,
myrrh and frankincense and gold.

3. Holy child, what gift of grace,
from the Father freely willed!
In your infant form we trace
all God's promises fulfilled.

4. Holy child, whose human years
span like ours delight and pain,
one in human joys and tears,
one in all but sin and stain.

5. Holy child, so far from home,
sons of men to seek and save,
to what dreadful death you come,
to what dark and silent grave!

6. Holy child, before whose name
powers of darkness faint and fall;
conquered, death and sin and shame,
Jesus Christ is Lord of all.

7. Holy child, how still you lie;
safe the manger, soft the hay,
clear upon the eastern sky
breaks the dawn of Christmas Day.

60

Derek Allan

Chorus:
Listen to the calypso for Christmas time,
the story of the coming of the child divine.
Listen how the Son of God came down to earth,
think about the wonder of his humble birth,
listen to the calypso for Christmas time.

1. Mary and Joseph, they leave their home town
and come to Bethlehem;
but they have got to sleep in a stable,
there is no room left for them.
Jesus is born and put in a manger,
somewhere for him to lie;
there he is warm and safe in the stable,
oxen and ass standing by.

Chorus:

2. Out in the fields the shepherds hear angels
singing about God's Son:
they speak of peace on earth and glad tidings
of joy to everyone.
They come to Mary and find the baby
just as the angels said:
here is the gift of God to mankind
asleep in his rough manger bed.
Chorus:

3. Wise men have seen a star in the east
and they come to seek a king.
Finding the baby they bow to Jesus
and make their rich offering.
Jesus is no more laid in a manger,
you will not find him there:
but he is waiting for you to put
the whole of your life in his care.
Chorus:

61

Captain Joy Webb

1. It was on a starry night when the hills were
bright,
earth lay sleeping, sleeping calm and still;
then in a cattle shed, in a manger bed,
a boy was born, king of all the world.
And all the angels sang for him,
the bells of heaven rang for him,
for a boy was born, king of all the world.
And all the angels sang for him,
the bells of heaven rang for him,
for a boy was born, king of all the world.

2. Soon the shepherds came that way, where the baby lay,
and were kneeling, kneeling by his side;
and their hearts believed again, for the peace of men,
for a boy was born, king of all the world.
And all the angels sang for him,
the bells of heaven rang for him,
for a boy was born, king of all the world.
And all the angels sang for him,
the bells of heaven rang for him,
for a boy was born, king of all the world.
On a starry night, on a starry night.

62

Blaine H Allen

1. Little baby Jesus, born in Bethlehem;
little baby Jesus, born in Bethlehem;
little baby Jesus, born to be –
the Saviour of the world for you and me;
little baby Jesus, born in Bethlehem.

2. Little baby Jesus, born in Bethlehem;
little baby Jesus, born in Bethlehem;
little baby Jesus, born to die,
to suffer on the cross for you and I;
little baby Jesus, born in Bethlehem.

3. Little baby Jesus, born in a stable bare;
little baby Jesus, lyin' in a manger there;
little baby Jesus, king to be,
the master of the earth, the sky and sea;
little baby Jesus, born in Bethlehem.

4. Little baby Jesus, born in Bethlehem;
little baby Jesus, born in Bethlehem;
little baby Jesus, do come in,
come right into my heart and save me from sin!
Little baby Jesus, born in Bethlehem.

63

Adapted from traditional words by David Evans

1. Mary had a baby,
yes, Lord,
Mary had a baby,
yes, my Lord,
Mary had a baby,
Chorus: *yes, Lord,*
the people came to Bethlehem
to see her Son.

2. What did she name him?
Yes, Lord,
what did she name him?
Yes, my Lord,
what did she name him?
Chorus:

3. She named him Jesus,
yes, Lord,
she named him Jesus,
yes, my Lord,
she named him Jesus,
Chorus:

4. Where was he born?
Yes, Lord,
where was he born?
Yes, my Lord,
where was he born?
Chorus:

5. Born in a stable,
yes, Lord,
born in a stable,
yes, my Lord,
born in a stable,
Chorus:

6. Where did she lay him?
Yes, Lord,
where did she lay him?
Yes, my Lord,
where did she lay him?
Chorus:

7. Laid him in a manger,
yes, Lord,
laid him in a manger,
yes, my Lord,
laid him in a manger,
Chorus:

64

Carolyn Gower

Chorus:

Nowell! Nowell! Nowell! Nowell!
Long, long ago in Bethlehem's stable,
laid in a cattle stall,
Jesus was born of lowly Mary,
Jesus who died for all.

Refrain:

Nowell! Nowell! Nowell! Nowell!
Jesus has come, the Saviour of all the world;
be glad!
Ring out the news of goodness and joy,
Jesus is born.

1. Angels sang the Christmas song,
sang it to humble shepherds,
told them a king had come.

Refrain:

2. Kings saw a star that shone so bright,
they followed it till at last,
o'er Bethlehem beamed its light.

Refrain:

3. Let us join with shepherds and kings
to tell the world of Jesus,
the peace and the joy that he brings.

Chorus:

Nowell, nowell, nowell, nowell;
Jesus is come, let us go and worship,
kneel by the cattle stall,
Jesus the child of lowly Mary,
born on Christmas morn.

Refrain:

65

Judy Davies

Chorus: *Play your pipe! Beat your drum!*
Sing to Christ the Saviour.
Come and worship, come and worship,
worship Christ our king.

1. Shepherds, come a-dancing, bring your pipe and drum,
come and see the baby, run, run, run!
Chorus:

2. Peaceful in the manger, see him lying there,
gently gather round him, O take care!
Chorus:

3. Listen to the angels, can you hear them sing?
Welcoming the Saviour, he's our king!
Chorus:

4. Come to us, Lord Jesus, come to us again,
in our hearts we'll keep you, there to reign!
Chorus:

66

Valerie Collison

1. When Mary came to Bethlehem
long ago,
she found no room inside the inn,
nowhere to go;
'We've no more space for trav'lers,
we have no room at all.
The best that we can offer is a cattle stall.'

Chorus: *Nowell, nowell, the angels sing,*
nowell, nowell, their voices ring,
nowell, nowell, we come and bring
our thanks and praise and homage
to a newborn king.

2. He did not have a royal crib,
this child divine,
he did not wear a silken robe,
nothing so fine!
He did not need a palace,
he did not seek a throne,
for all the world around him was his very own!

Chorus:

3. The shepherds came to worship him,
Jesus the Lord,
the wise men brought their precious gifts
with one accord;
we too would come and worship
our Saviour and our King,
to you, O Lord, our loving hearts we gladly
bring.

Chorus:

67 *Translated from a Gascon carol*

1. Winds through the olive trees
softly did blow
round little Bethlehem,
long, long ago.
Sheep on the hillside lay
white as the snow;
shepherds were watching them,
long, long ago.

2. Then from the happy skies
angels bent low,
singing their songs of joy,
long, long ago.
For in his manger bed
cradled we know,
Christ came to Bethlehem,
long, long ago.

2. When Jesus lived on earth

68 *Unknown*

1. A workman in a village home,
he toiled for daily bread,
he spent his strength in honest work,
with hands and heart and head.
A king uncrowned, though no man knew,
kingly he lived, and true.

2. He healed the deaf, the dumb, the blind,
the maimed, the sick, the sad;
he gave to them his Father's strength,
the radiant strength he had.
They followed him, a king uncrowned,
new life with him they found.

3. He rode into Jerusalem,
they hailed him, 'David's Son,'
yet, when in danger of his life,
they left him, every one.
Though crowned with thorns and crucified,
as Lord and king he died.

4. O King uncrowned, Leader of men,
O Captain, brave and true,
we praise you for your kingly life;
we would be kingly too.
To serve you now, O Saviour King,
our lives to you we bring.

69

Jancis Harvey

Chorus:
From the darkness came light,
from the blackest of nights;
wait for the morning, the sunlight, the dawning;
from the darkness came light.

1. Earth so dark and so cold, what great secrets you hold;
the promise of spring, the wonder you bring,
the beauty of nature unfolds.
Chorus:

2. Jesus was born in a stall, born to bring light to us all.
He came to love us, a new life to give us;
Jesus was born in a stall.
Chorus:

3. Jesus died on Calvary, suffered for you and me;
he rose from the dark and gloom, out of a stony tomb,
walked in the world and was free.
Chorus:

4. We have this new life to share, a love to pass on everywhere;
time spent in giving, a joy in our living,
in showing to others we care.
Chorus:

70

Unknown

Here comes Jesus, see him walking on the
water,
he'll lift you up and he'll help you to stand.
Here comes Jesus, he's the master of the waves
that roll.
Here comes Jesus, he'll make you whole.

71

J M Neale verses 1 & 2
Percy Dearmer verses 3 & 4

1. Jesus, good above all other,
gentle child of gentle mother;
in a stable born our brother,
whom the angel hosts adore.

2. Jesus, cradled in a manger,
keep us free from sin and danger;
and to all, both friend and stranger,
give your blessing evermore.

3. Jesus, for your people dying,
risen Master, death defying;
Lord of heaven, your grace supplying,
come to us – be present here!

4. Lord, in all our doings guide us,
pride and hate shall not divide us;
we'll go on with you beside us,
and with joy we'll persevere.

72

Margaret Cropper

1. Jesus' hands were kind hands, doing good to all,
healing pain and sickness, blessing children
small;

washing tired feet, and saving those who fall;
Jesus' hands were kind hands, doing good to all.

2. Take my hands, Lord Jesus, let them work for you;
make them strong and gentle, kind in all I do;
let me watch you, Jesus, till I'm gentle too,
till my hands are kind hands, quick to work for you.

73

Roger Jones

Chorus:
Jesus rode a donkey into town.
Many folks turned out from miles around.
What a sight to see, a man to set men free,
riding on a donkey into town.

1. Jesus, is it true the things the people say of you?
Did you really make a blind man see?
And if all I've heard about you turns out to be true,
can you really do the same for me?
Chorus:

2. Tell me do you think he'll take the Roman guards by storm?
Do you think he'll show the priests the door?
Wonder if he's pleased by all the shouting from the crowd,
even by the palms upon the floor.
Chorus:

Descant to final chorus:
Hosanna, hosanna, blessed is the man
that cometh in the name, cometh in the name
of the Lord!

74

Translated from Urdu by
Dermott Monahan

1. Jesus the Lord said: 'I am the bread,
the bread of life for mankind am I,
the bread of life for mankind am I,
the bread of life for mankind am I.'
Jesus the Lord said: 'I am the bread,
the bread of life for mankind am I.'

2. Jesus the Lord said: 'I am the way,
the true and living way am I,
the true and living way am I,
the true and living way am I.'
Jesus the Lord said: 'I am the way,
the true and living way am I.'

3. Jesus the Lord said: 'I am the light,
the one true light of the world am I,
the one true light of the world am I,
the one true light of the world am I.'
Jesus the Lord said: 'I am the light,
the one true light of the world am I.'

4. Jesus the Lord said: 'I am the shepherd,
the one good shepherd of the sheep am I,
the one good shepherd of the sheep am I,
the one good shepherd of the sheep am I.'
Jesus the Lord said: 'I am the shepherd,
the one good shepherd of the sheep am I.'

5. Jesus the Lord said: 'I am the life,
the resurrection and the life am I,
the resurrection and the life am I,
the resurrection and the life am I.'
Jesus the Lord said: 'I am the life,
the resurrection and the life am I.'

75

June Wright

1. Jesus was baptised in Jordan
in the crowd like other men.
John the Baptist bowed before him:
'Look! Here is the promised one!
Now I see God's great plan.
You are Christ, and you are man!'

2. Jesus called to John and Peter;
'Fish for people, work for me,
leave your boats and leave your fish nets!'
They replied immediately:
'Now we see God's great plan.
You want us, and you want all men!'

3. Jesus saw the people suffer,
sick and lame and deaf and blind.
'Come stand up, be strong and cheerful!
Healthy body, healthy mind!
God loves you, loves all men!'
This is what he said to them.

4. Jesus saw the people hating,
saw their cruelty, felt their tears.
Taught them how to live like brothers,
helped them overcome their fears.
'Love your God, love all men!'
This is what he said to them.

76

Pat Uhl Howard

Chorus:
O what a gift! What a wonderful gift!
Who can tell the wonders of the Lord?
Let us open our eyes and our ears and our hearts;
it is Christ the Lord it is he!

1. In the stillness of the night
when the world was asleep,
the almighty Word leapt out.
He came to Mary, he came to us,
Christ came to the land of Galilee.
Christ our Lord and our king!
Chorus:

2. On the night before he died –
it was Passover night
and he gathered his friends together.
He broke the bread, he blessed the wine;
it was the gift of his love and his life.
Christ our Lord and our king!
Chorus:

3. On the hill of Calvary
while the world held its breath,
it was there for us all to see;
God gave his Son, his only Son,
for the love of you and me.
Christ our Lord and our king!
Chorus:

4. It was early on that morning
when the guards were asleep,
back to life came he!
He conquered death, he conquered sin,
but victory he gave to you and me.
Christ our Lord and our king!

Chorus:

5. Some day with the saints
we will come before our Father,
and then we will shout and dance and sing!
For in our midst for our eyes to see
will be Christ our Lord and our king.
Christ our Lord and our king!

Chorus:

77

Geoffrey Curtis

1. There's a child in the streets
gives joy to all he meets,
full of life, with many friends,
works and plays till daylight ends.

Chorus: *There's a man for all the people,*
a man whose love is true.
May this man for all the people –
help me love others too.

2. There's a preacher in a crowd
shouts to fishermen out loud,
'Leave your boats and leave the sea,
come along and work with me.'

Chorus:

3. There's a teacher tells a tale,
makes men argue without fail,
some are angry, some agree,
when he says, 'You follow me.'
Chorus:

4. There's a leader at a feast,
but he says that he's the least,
rolls his sleeves to wash their feet,
breaks the bread and tells them, 'Eat.'
Chorus:

5. There's a prisoner on a cross
and his friends weep for their loss,
but a soldier with a sword
says, 'This man has come from God.'
Chorus:

6. There's a voice inside a room,
'I have risen from the tomb,
I am bringing you God's peace
and your joy will never cease.'
Chorus:

78

Geoffrey Marshall-Taylor

1. There is singing in the desert, there is laughter
in the skies,
there are wise men filled with wonder, there
are shepherds with surprise,
you can tell the world is dancing by the light
that's in their eyes,
for Jesus Christ is here.

Chorus: *Come and sing aloud your praises,*
come and sing aloud your praises,
come and sing aloud your praises,
for Jesus Christ is here.

2. He hears deaf men by the lakeside, he sees blind men in the streets,
he goes up to those who cannot walk, he talks to all he meets,
touching silken robes or tattered clothes, it's everyone he greets,
for Jesus Christ is here.
Chorus:

3. There is darkness on the hillside, there is sorrow in the town,
there's a man upon a wooden cross, a man who's gazing down,
you can see the marks of love and not the furrows of a frown,
for Jesus Christ is here.
Chorus:

4. There is singing in the desert, there is laughter in the skies,
there are wise men filled with wonder, there are shepherds with surprise,
you can tell the world is dancing by the light that's in their eyes,
for Jesus Christ is here.
Chorus:

79

Edward J Burns

1. We have a gospel to proclaim,
good news for men in all the earth;
the gospel of a Saviour's name:
we sing his glory, tell his worth.

2. Tell of his birth at Bethlehem,
not in a royal house or hall
but in a stable dark and dim,
the Word made flesh, a light for all.

3. Tell of his death at Calvary,
hated by those he came to save,
in lonely suffering on the cross;
for all he loved his life he gave.

4. Tell of that glorious Easter morn:
empty the tomb, for he was free.
He broke the power of death and hell
that we might share his victory.

5. Tell of his reign at God's right hand,
by all creation glorified.
He sends his Spirit on his church
to live for him, the Lamb who died.

6. Now we rejoice to name him King:
Jesus is Lord of all the earth.
This gospel-message we proclaim:
we sing his glory, tell his worth.

80 *Unknown*

What *love! God gave us his Son,
what love, God gave us his Son,
what love, God gave us his Son,
what love, what love, God gave us his Son,
what love, what love, God gave us his Son.

2. What *love! He died on the cross . . .

3. What *love! He rose from the grave . . .

4. What *love! He's coming again . . .

5. What *love! Alleluia!

*or '*grace*'.

81

Valerie Collison

1. Who was once a child like me,
running, jumping, glad and free,
happy just a child to be?
It's Jesus!
He loved creatures great and small,
flowers fair and mountains tall,
taught his Father's care for all –
this Jesus!

2. Who turned water into wine,
bade the needy come and dine?
'You can be a friend of mine,'
said Jesus.
He could heal the blind and lame,
wicked men could put to shame,
children praised his holy name –
it's Jesus!

3. Who's that hanging on a tree,
dying there for you and me?
Only one man could it be –
that's Jesus!
Now he's risen from the tomb,
chased away all fear and gloom,
and in heaven for me there's room
with Jesus!

3. When Jesus died

82

Unknown

1. God is so good,
God is so good,
God is so good –
he's so good to me.

2. He took my sin,
he took my sin,
he took my sin –
he's so good to me.

3. Now I am free,
now I am free,
now I am free –
he's so good to me.

4. God is so good,
he took my sin,
now I am free,
he's so good to me.

83

Carole Pegler

Chorus: *My Lord loves me*
and oh, the wonder I see!
A rainbow shines in my window:
my Lord loves me.

1. He died for me,
on a cross at Calvary,
he bore my sin and my shame
when he died for me.

Chorus:

84

S Crossman
Jubilate Hymns version

1. My song is love unknown,
my Saviour's love for me;
love to the loveless shown
that they might lovely be:
but who am I, that for my sake
my Lord should take frail flesh and die?

2. He came from heaven's throne
salvation to bestow;
but men refused, and none
the longed-for Christ would know:
this is my friend, my friend indeed,
who at my need his life did spend.

3. Sometimes they crowd his way
and his sweet praises sing,
resounding all the day
hosannas to their king:
then 'crucify' is all their breath,
and for his death they thirst and cry.

4. Why, what has my Lord done
to cause this rage and spite?
He made the lame to run,
and gave the blind their sight:
what injuries! Yet these are why
the Lord most high so cruelly dies.

5. With angry shouts, they have
my dear Lord done away;
a murderer they save,
the prince of life they slay!
Yet willingly he bears the shame
that through his name all might be free.

6. Here might I stay and sing
of him my soul adores;
never was love, dear King,
never was grief like yours!
This is my friend in whose sweet praise
I all my days could gladly spend.

85

David Mowbray

1. O Christ, the Master Carpenter,
high on a cross you died;
a wooden cross, with iron nails,
a spear thrust in your side.

2. O Christ, upon that Friday cross
your work for man was done;
yet, truly, in my life today
your work has just begun.

3. O Christ, take up your workman's tools
and shape my life anew,
that I who now appear rough-hewn
may be restored by you.

4. O Christ, the Master Carpenter,
let beauty gently shine
within the workshop of my life –
the praise be yours, not mine.

86 *Valerie Collison*

1. Why did Jesus suffer so
on a cross of shame?
All the hatred men could know
heaped on him the blame;
cruel nails and crown of thorn,
heartache, pain, and bitter scorn,
all by Jesus bravely borne,
just for you and me!

2. Jesus suffered in my place
on that cross of shame;
he who set the world in space
took for me the blame;
just to show his love for me,
and from sin to set me free,
Jesus died upon the tree,
just for you and me!

3. I'm so glad that Jesus rose
that first Easter Day;
now I know that Jesus lives
in the world today!
He will hear me when I call,
he will keep me lest I fall,
he's the greatest friend of all,
just for you and me!

4. *When Jesus came alive again*

87

Charles Wesley

Christ the Lord is risen today.
Alleluia!
We will praise the Lord and say –
alleluia!
Now he lives no more to die.
Alleluia!
We will sing our praises high –
alleluia!

88

Unknown

He is Lord, he is Lord,
he is risen from the dead,
and he is Lord!
Every knee shall bow,
every tongue confess
that Jesus Christ is Lord.

89

C A Alington

1. Good Christians all, rejoice and sing!
Now is the triumph of our king;
to all the world glad news we bring:
Alleluia, alleluia, alleluia!

2. The Lord of life is risen today;
death's mighty stone is rolled away;
let all mankind rejoice and say,
'Alleluia, alleluia, alleluia!'

3. We praise in songs of victory
that love, that life, which cannot die,
and sing with hearts uplifted high,
'Alleluia, alleluia, alleluia!'

4. Your name we bless, O risen Lord,
and sing today with one accord
the life laid down, the life restored:
Alleluia, alleluia, alleluia!

90

Roland Meredith

1. Our eyes have seen the glory of our Saviour, Christ the Lord;
he's seated at his Father's side in love and full accord;
from there upon the sons of men his Spirit is out-poured,
all hail, ascended King!

Chorus: *Glory, glory, hallelujah,*
glory, glory, hallelujah,
glory, glory, hallelujah,
all hail, ascended King!

2. He came to earth at Christmas and was made a man like us;
he taught, he healed, he suffered – and they nailed him to the cross;
he rose again on Easter Day – our Lord victorious,
all hail, ascended King!

Chorus:

3. The good news of his kingdom must be
preached to every shore,
the news of peace and pardon, and the end of
strife and war;
the secret of his kingdom is to serve him
evermore,
all hail, ascended King!
Chorus:

4. His kingdom is a family of men of every race,
they live their lives in harmony, enabled by his
grace;
they follow his example till they see him face to
face,
all hail, ascended King!
Chorus:

91

W H Hamilton

1. When Easter to the dark world came,
fair flowers glowed like scarlet flame:
Chorus: *At Eastertide, at Eastertide,*
O glad was the world at Eastertide.

2. When Mary in the garden walked,
and with her risen master talked:
Chorus:

3. When John and Peter in their gloom
met angels at the empty tomb:
Chorus:

4. When Thomas' heart with grief was black,
Then Jesus like a king came back:
Chorus:

5. And friend to friend in wonder said:
'The Lord is risen from the dead!'
Chorus:

6. This Eastertide with joyful voice
we'll sing 'The Lord is king! Rejoice!'
At Eastertide, at Eastertide,
O sing, all the world, for Eastertide.

92

Fred Pratt Green

1. This joyful Eastertide,
what need is there for grieving?
Cast all your care aside
and be not unbelieving.

Chorus: *Come, share our Easter joy*
that death could not imprison,
nor any power destroy,
our Christ, who is arisen,
arisen, arisen, arisen!

2. No work for him is vain,
no faith in him mistaken,
for Easter makes it plain
his kingdom is not shaken.
Chorus:

3. Then put your trust in Christ,
in waking or in sleeping.
His grace on earth sufficed;
he'll never quit his keeping.
Chorus:

93

E L Budry, trs. R B Hoyle
Jubilate Hymns version

1. Yours be the glory! Risen, conquering Son;
endless is the victory over death you won;
angels robed in splendour rolled the stone
away,
kept the folded grave clothes
where your body lay:
Chorus:
Yours be the glory! Risen, conquering Son:
endless is the victory over death you won.

2. See! Jesus meets us, risen from the tomb,
lovingly he greets us, scatters fear and gloom;
let the church with gladness
hymns of triumph sing,
for her Lord is living, death has lost its sting:
Chorus:

3. No more we doubt you, glorious prince of life:
what is life without you? Aid us in our strife;
make us more than conquerors,
through your deathless love,
bring us safe through Jordan to your home
above:
Chorus:

5. *When Jesus comes again*

94

Christopher Porteous

1. Bethlehem waiting,
Joseph and Mary,
finding a stable,
sleep in the hay.
Angels are singing,
shepherds are watching,
Jesus is sleeping,
joyful the day.

2. Valleys shall echo,
hung between mountains,
shaken with thunder,
covered with snow.
Satan is conquered,
evil is broken,
Jesus has risen,
worship the day.

3. Souls are awaking,
clouds are descending,
sunshine is breaking,
clouds melt away.
Promise fulfilling,
Jesus returning,
raising the living,
soon is the day.

4. Sorrow and sighing,
seen in our faces,
anguish and dying,
banished away.
Christians are rising,
glory is waiting,
Jesus is coming,
watch for the day.

95

M V Old

Jesus will come once more.
Jesus will come once more.
He'll return and ev'ryone will know he's king!
king! king!
King over all, he'll reign!
King over all, he'll reign!
He'll return and ev'ryone will know he's king!
king! king!

96

Jim Punton

1. Oh, when the Lord shall come to reign,
oh, when the Lord shall come to reign,
we're gonna be among his people,
when the Lord shall come to reign.

2. And when they shout the Saviour's praise,
and when they shout the Saviour's praise,
we're gonna be among his people,
when they shout the Saviour's praise.

3. And when with joy creation rings,
and when with joy creation rings,
we're gonna be among his people,
when with joy creation rings.

97

M V Old

When Jesus moved beyond our sight,
in heaven to live and reign,
he told his friends to spread his word
until he comes again.
Lord Jesus, you'll return to earth
in glorious power to bring
an end to evil, and we'll see
the world acclaim you King.

THE HOLY SPIRIT

98

Unknown

1. All over the world the Spirit is moving,
all over the world as the prophet said it would be;
all over the world there's a mighty revelation
of the glory of the Lord, as the waters cover the sea.

2. All over his church God's Spirit is moving,
all over his church as the prophet said it would be;
all over his church there's a mighty revelation
of the glory of the Lord, as the waters cover the sea.

3. Right here in this place the Spirit is moving,
right here in this place as the prophet said it would be;
right here in this place there's a mighty revelation
of the glory of the Lord, as the waters cover the sea.

99

Unknown

Jesus, Jesus,
let me tell you what I know!
You have given us your Spirit;
we love you so.

100

Alda M Milner-Barry

1. It is the Holy Spirit's day,
sing joyful alleluia!
When all Christ's people met to pray;
sing joyful alleluia!

2. With rushing sound, with heav'nly flame
on them the Holy Spirit came:
they blessed and praised God's glorious name;
sing joyful alleluia!

101

Christopher Idle

Chorus:
Spirit of holiness, wisdom and faithfulness,
wind of the Lord, blowing strongly and free:
strength of our serving
and joy of our worshipping –
Spirit of God, bring your fulness to me!

1. You came to interpret and teach us effectively
all that the Saviour has spoken and done;
to glorify Jesus is all your activity –
promise and gift of the Father and Son.
Chorus:

2. You came with your gifts to supply all our
poverty,
pouring your love on the church in her need;
you came with your fruit for our growth to
maturity,
richly refreshing the souls that you feed.
Chorus:

102

Jane & Betsy Clowe

Chorus:
Wind of God, blow on me; wind of God, set me free,
wind of God, my Father sent the blessed Holy Spirit.

1. Jesus told us all about you,
how we could not live without you,
with his blood the power bought
to help us live the life he taught.
Chorus:

2. When we're weary you console us,
when we're lonely you enfold us,
when in danger you uphold us,
blessed Holy Spirit.
Chorus:

3. When into the church you came,
it was not in your own but Jesus' name:
Jesus Christ is still the same –
he sends the Holy Spirit.
Chorus:

4. Set us free to love our brothers,
set us free to live for others,
that the world the Son might see
and Jesus' name exalted be.
Chorus:

WHAT GOD WANTS OF US

103

Unknown

One step more, one step more,
give me faith for one step more,
one step more, my Saviour, one step more,
faith for one step more.
Though the way is weary,
and the day is dark and drear,
never fear, he is near.
Dark and drear may be the way
but hear my Saviour say,
'Follow me! Follow me!'

104

C R Vaughan

1. From the distant east and the farthest west,
I will bring my people home.
Let my people return from the distant lands,
I will bring my people home.

Chorus: *Someone is shouting in the desert,*
'Prepare a road for the Lord;
make a path straight for him to travel!
Prepare a road for the Lord.
Turn away from your sins.'

2. Do not cling to the past or the long ago,
I will bring my people home.
I will make a road and the rivers flow;
I will bring my people home.

Chorus:

3. Do not be afraid, through the waters deep
I will bring my people home.
Do not be afraid, as you pass through fire,
I will bring my people home.

Someone is shouting in the desert,
'Prepare a road for the Lord;
make a path straight for him to travel!
Prepare a road for the Lord.
Turn away from your sins.
Turn away from your sins.
Turn away from your sins.'

105

Geoffrey Marshall-Taylor

1. Can you be sure that the rain will fall?
Can you be sure that birds will fly?
Can you be sure that rivers will flow?
Or that the sun will light the sky?

Chorus: *God has promised.*
God never breaks a promise he makes.
His word is always true.

2. Can you be sure that the tide will turn?
Can you be sure that grass will grow?
Can you be sure that night will come,
or that the sun will melt the snow?

Chorus:

3. You can be sure that God is near;
you can be sure he won't let you down;
you can be sure he'll always hear;
and that he's given Jesus, his Son.

Chorus:

106

Diane Davis Andrew

1. God has called . . . . (name), he will not fail . . . . (him, her), } *3 times*
so trust in God and obey him.

2. God has called you, he will not fail you, } *3 times*
so trust in God and obey him.

3. God has called us, we will not fail him, } *3 times*
so trust in God and obey him. (repeat)

107

Derek Haylock

1. I'm going to knock, knock, knock, knock,
knockity knock,
to find out why and what and where.
I'm going to knock, knock, knock, knock,
knockity knock,
till the voice of God I hear.
Knock and it will be opened,
ask and you will receive,
seek and you will certainly find,
these promises I believe.
(I believe in them).

2. I'm going to knock, knock, knock, knock,
knockity knock,
until the truth is clear in my mind.
I'm going to knock, knock, knock, knock,
knockity knock,
till the Saviour's love I find.

Jesus is also knocking,
waiting to be let in.
He who died to save us all
will cleanse you from your sin.
(If you let him in).

3. Knock, knock, knock, knock, knockity knock,
he waits for you to do your part,
hear his knock, knock, knock, knock, knockity knock,
and welcome him into your heart.

108

Unknown

1. I have decided to follow Jesus,
I have decided to follow Jesus,
I have decided to follow Jesus;
no turning back, no turning back.

2. The cross before me, the world behind me,
the cross before me, the world behind me,
the cross before me, the world behind me;
no turning back, no turning back.

109

Sydney Carter

1. One more step along the world I go,
one more step along the world I go.
From the old things to the new
keep me travelling along with you.

Chorus:
And it's from the old I travel to the new,
keep me travelling along with you.

2. Round the corner of the world I turn,
more and more about the world I learn.
All the new things that I see
you'll be looking at along with me.
Chorus:

3. As I travel through the bad and good
keep me travelling the way I should.
Where I see no way to go
you'll be telling me the way, I know.
Chorus:

4. Give me courage when the world is rough,
keep me loving though the world is tough.
Leap and sing in all I do,
keep me travelling along with you.
Chorus:

5. You are older than the world can be,
you are younger than the life in me.
Ever old and ever new,
keep me travelling along with you.
Chorus:

110

Captain Joy Webb

1. Oh, if you set out for the City of Light,
then you must follow, must follow, must
follow.
You must never let the master out of your sight,
you must follow, must follow, must follow.

Chorus:
Oh, you're sure to get there by faith and pray'r,
if you follow, you follow, you follow.
Oh, you're sure to get there, if you just keep
a-following on.
Follow la la la la la, (4 times)
follow, follow, follow, follow.

2. Oh, if you want to see what the saints have
seen,
then you must follow, must follow, must
follow.
You must keep on the pathway where they
have been.
You must follow, must follow, must follow.
Chorus:

3. Oh, there's sure to be a time when you want to
turn back,
then you must follow, must follow, must
follow.
Just keep right on that straight and narrow
track.
You must follow, must follow, must follow.
Chorus:

4. Oh, come now, get started, there's no time to
lose,
then you must follow, must follow, must
follow.
Two ways are set before you, but you have to
choose,
you must follow, must follow, must follow.
Chorus:

111

Mary Smail

1. Prepare the way of the Lord!
Make his paths straight;
open the gates that he may enter freely
into our lives.
Hosanna! We cry to the Lord.

Chorus:
And we will fill the earth
with the sound of his praise –
Jesus is Lord! Let him be adored!
Yes, we will have this man to reign over us.
Hosanna! We follow the Lord.

2. And he will come to us as he came before,
clothed in his grace, to stand in our place;
and we behold him, now our priest and our king.
Hosanna! We sing to the Lord.

Chorus:

3. Prepare the way of the Lord!
Make his paths straight;
open the gates that he may enter freely
into our lives.
Hosanna! We cry to the Lord.

Chorus:

112

Peter Lewis

Chorus: *Sing life, sing love, sing Jesus,*
sing out wherever you are;
sing life, sing love, sing Jesus,
sing out whoever you are.

1. Life is a gift we can use or abuse,
life can be great or a bore.
It all depends on the way that we choose,
whether we notice or just ignore
God's love.

Chorus:

2. Love is something we can give or can take.
Love can bring life or bring death.
I can love myself and be on the make,
or live for others till my last breath
like Jesus.

Chorus:

3. Jesus gives life and in love Jesus died,
Jesus the Truth and the Way.
And although he is betrayed and denied,
in men his life and love live on
today.

Chorus:

113

Valerie Collison

1. The journey of life may be easy, may be hard,
there'll be dangers on the way;
with Christ at my side I'll do battle as I ride
'gainst the foe that would lead me astray.

Chorus:
Will you ride, ride, ride with the King of Kings,
will you follow my leader true;
will you shout hosanna to the lowly Son of God,
who died for me and you.

2. My burden is light and a song is in my heart,
as I travel on life's way;
for Christ is my Lord and he's given me his word,
that by my side he'll stay.

Chorus:

3. When doubts arise and when tears are in my eyes,
when all seems lost to me;
with Christ as my guide I can smile whate'er betide,
for he my strength will be.

Chorus:

4. I'll follow my leader wherever he may go,
for Jesus is my friend;
he'll lead me on to the place where he has gone,
when I come to my journey's end.

Chorus:

114

Robert Stoodley

1. Who does Jesus love,
Jesus love, Jesus love?
Who does Jesus love?
He loves everyone!
Well, ev'rybody should love Jesus, should love Jesus.
Ev'rybody should love Jesus too!

2. Who does Jesus care for,
Jesus care for, Jesus care for?
Who does Jesus care for?
He cares for everyone.
Well, ev'rybody should care for Jesus, (etc.)

3. Who did Jesus come to serve,
come to serve, come to serve?
Who did Jesus come to serve?
He came to serve ev'ryone.
Well, ev'rybody should serve Jesus, (etc.)

4. What did Jesus say,
Jesus say, Jesus say?
What did Jesus say?
He said love everyone.
Well, ev'rybody should love each other, (etc.)

5. Who did Jesus die for,
Jesus die for, Jesus die for?
Who did Jesus die for?
He died for everyone.
Well, ev'rybody should live for Jesus, (etc.)

LIVING AS GOD'S FRIENDS

115

Adapted from 'St Patrick's Breastplate'
by James Quinn

1. Christ be beside me,
Christ be before me,
Christ be behind me,
king of my heart.
Christ be within me,
Christ be below me,
Christ be above me,
never to part.

2. Christ on my right hand,
Christ on my left hand,
Christ all around me,
shield in the strife.
Christ in my sleeping,
Christ in my sitting,
Christ in my rising,
light of my life.

3. Christ be in all hearts
thinking about me,
Christ be in all tongues
telling of me.
Christ be the vision
in eyes that see me,
in ears that hear me,
Christ ever be.

116

From The Lord's Prayer
James E Seddon

1. Father God in heaven,
Lord most high:
hear your children's prayer,
Lord most high:
hallowed be your name,
Lord most high –
O Lord, hear our prayer.

2. May your kingdom come
here on earth;
may your will be done
here on earth,
as it is in heaven
so on earth –
O Lord, hear our prayer.

3. Give us daily bread
day by day,
and forgive our sins
day by day,
as we too forgive
day by day –
O Lord, hear our prayer.

4. Lead us in your way,
make us strong;
when temptations come
make us strong;
save us from all sin,
keep us strong –
O Lord, hear our prayer.

5. All things come from you,
all are yours –
kingdom, glory, power,
all are yours;
take our lives and gifts,
all are yours –
O Lord, hear our prayer.

117

Timothy Dudley-Smith

1. Christ be my leader by night as by day;
safe through the darkness, for he is the way.
Gladly I follow, my future his care,
darkness is daylight when Jesus is there.

2. Christ be my teacher in age as in youth,
drifting or doubting, for he is the truth.
Grant me to trust him; though shifting as sand,
doubt cannot daunt me; in Jesus I stand.

3. Christ be my Saviour in calm as in strife;
death cannot hold me, for he is the life.
Not darkness nor doubting nor sin and its stain
can touch my salvation: with Jesus I reign.

118

Susan McClellan, John Pac and Keith Ryecroft

1. Colours of day dawn into the mind,
the sun has come up, the night is behind.
Go down in the city, into the street,
and let's give the message to the people we meet.

Chorus:
So light up the fire and let the flame burn,
open the door, let Jesus return.
Take seeds of his Spirit, let the fruit grow,
tell the people of Jesus, let his love show.

2. Go through the park, on into the town;
the sun still shines on, it never goes down.
The light of the world is risen again;
the people of darkness are needing our friend.
Chorus:

3. Open your eyes, look into the sky,
the darkness has come, the sun came to die.
The evening draws on, the sun disappears,
but Jesus is living, his Spirit is near.
Chorus:

119

C R Vaughan

1. Do not judge others, and God will not judge
you;
don't condemn others, and God won't
condemn you;
forgive the others, and God will forgive you;
give to others, and God will give to you.
Chorus:
Speck, speck, speck in your brother's eye,
log, log, log in your own eye,
eye, eye, eye, eye;
take the log out of your own eye, eye,
to see the speck, speck, speck in your brother's
eye.

2. Ask, and you will receive, seek and you will find;
knock, and the door will be opened from behind.
Do for the others what you want them to do;
give to others, and God will give to you.
Chorus:

3. Would you give a stone when your son asks for bread?
Or give a snake when he asks for fish instead?
Bad as you are, you know how to give the good;
give to others, and God will give to you.
Chorus:

120

Derek Haylock

I'm going to build for Jesus a life of praise,
a life of faith which follows his ways;
a life which hears his teaching and obeys,
a life of love and praise!
There is no other foundation that can be laid
as sure as the one which God has made,
in giving Jesus, the rock on which to base
a life of love and praise.

Jesus, always the same, faithful and true,
his promises sure.
Jesus, trusting his name, my life will be secure,
and full of love and joy and peace and hope and praise;

I'm going to build for Jesus a life of praise;
a life of faith which follows his ways;
a life which hears his teaching and obeys,
a life of love and praise to Jesus,
I'm building a life of praise.

121

Diane Davis Andrew

Chorus:
I'm not alone for my Father is with me,
with me wherever I go.
Speaking words of faith, of courage and of love,
he's with me, he loves me wherever I go.

1. Waking in the morning,
getting ready for school,
walking down the road,
in class, at work, or at play,
he's with me, he loves me wherever I go.
Chorus:

2. And when I find myself in a mess,
I can trust in him,
call on his name and watch him move,
he's with me, he loves me wherever I go.
Chorus:

3. All of my life ev'rywhere that I go,
I will walk with him,
praising him and blessing his name,
he's with me, he loves me wherever I go.
Chorus: (repeat last line)

122

John Lane

1. It really is a worry
to stop and look around;
there's sadness, hate and madness,
a world that's upside down!
But Jesus built a kingdom,
he came to set it up;
there's goodness, love and justice,
a kingdom right side up!

Chorus:
Right side up! It's a brand new way to live.
When others say 'Get even' Jesus says 'Forgive!'
Right side up! His love is in our hearts,
he'll take out the hate and we'll make a new start.

2. When people say, 'Fight harder!'
he says, 'Make peace instead!'
When people say, 'Act smarter!'
he says, 'Be true instead!'
When people grasp possessions,
he says, 'Be kind instead!'
When people sigh, 'Life's hopeless,'
he says, 'Tell God instead.'

Chorus:

3. When people say, 'Look after
number one and get ahead!'
then Jesus says, 'Be happy;
obey God's ways instead!'
When people say, 'It's nonsense!'
keep right on Jesus' way.
His kingdom lasts forever –
it's here with us today.

Chorus:

123

George W Cooke

1. I have the joy, joy, joy, joy, down in my heart,
down in my heart, down in my heart,
I have the joy, joy, joy, joy, down in my heart,
down in my heart to stay.

2. I have the peace that passes understanding,
down in my heart,
down in my heart, down in my heart,
I have the peace that passes understanding,
down in my heart,
down in my heart to stay.

3. I have the love of Jesus, love of Jesus, down in
my heart,
down in my heart, down in my heart,
I have the love of Jesus, love of Jesus, down in
my heart,
down in my heart to stay.

124

Unknown

Joy[1] is the flag flown high from the castle[2] of my
heart[3],
from the castle[2] of my heart[3], from the castle[2] of
my heart[3].
Joy[1] is the flag flown high from the castle[2] of my
heart[3].
when the king[4] is in residence there[3].
So[1] let it fly in the sky, let[5] the whole world
know,

let[5] the whole world know, let[5] the whole world know.
So[1] let it fly in the sky, let[5] the whole world know
that the king[4] is in residence there[3].

Actions

1. *Arms raised, wave from side to side*
2. *Arms in roof shape above head*
3. *Point to heart*
4. *One finger pointed up*
5. *Arms up and draw a globe shape*

125

Traditional

1. Lord, I want to be like Jesus in my home,
in my home.
Lord, I want to be like Jesus in my home,
in my home, in my home;
Lord, I want to be like Jesus in my home.

2. Lord, I want to be like Jesus in my church,
in my church.
Lord, I want to be like Jesus in my church,
in my church, in my church;
Lord, I want to be like Jesus in my church.

3. Lord, I want to be like Jesus in my school,
in my school.
Lord, I want to be like Jesus in my school,
in my school, in my school;
Lord, I want to be like Jesus in my school.

126

Patrick Appleford

1. O Lord, all the world belongs to you,
and you are always making all things new.
What is wrong you forgive,
and the new life you give
is what's turning the world upside down.

2. The world's only loving to its friends,
but you have brought us love that never ends;
loving enemies too,
and this loving with you
is what's turning the world upside down.

3. This world lives divided and apart.
You draw all men together and we start
in your body to see
that in fellowship we
can be turning the world upside down.

4. The world wants the wealth to live in state,
but you show us a new way to be great:
like a servant you came,
and if we do the same,
we'll be turning the world upside down.

5. O Lord, all the world belongs to you,
and you are always making all things new.
Send your Spirit on all
in your church whom you call
to be turning the world upside down.

127

Fred Pratt Green

1. Once upon a time they went,
king and page together,
on a deed of kindness bent,
in the winter weather.
Every legend has its truth,
may this one remind us
where a neighbour is in need
Christ expects to find us.

2. Victims of injustice cry:
on your own confession
charity is not enough,
we must end oppression.
Yet, in such a world as this,
daily we are proving
there are evils none can cure
without deeds of loving.

3. We must follow in his steps
who was found in fashion
as a man, yet never lost
his divine compassion.
Lord, release such love in us,
we shall be more ready
to reach out with speedy aid
to your poor and needy.

128

Evelyn Tarner

Rejoice in the Lord always and again I say
rejoice. (*repeat*)
Rejoice, rejoice, and again I say rejoice,
rejoice, rejoice and again I say rejoice.

129

Judy Davies

1. Put your hand in your neighbour's hand,
and help him to carry his load;
neither pass him by, nor ignore his cry,
as you travel along life's road:
for Christ on the cross is the bridge between
my neighbour and me and my friend across the sea,
and all God's people are one in him,
and all God's people are one.

2. Put your hand in the Saviour's hand
as you venture into the night;
for the power of the Lord and his living word
shall be to your path a light:
for Christ on the cross is the bridge whereby
a man may reach up to his Father on high,
and all God's people are one in him,
and all God's people are one.

3. Hand in hand let us pledge our love
in the name of the crucified
for all those who are kin 'neath the colour of skin
though the oceans may still divide:
for Christ on the cross is the bridge between
my Father and me and my friend across the sea,
and all God's people are one in him,
and all God's people are one.

130

M V Old

Chorus: *Talk to God and share with him*
the thoughts you have each day.
Let him know what's on your mind –
he loves to hear you pray.

1. With 'Sorry', 'Please' and 'Thank you',
there's such a lot to say.
God loves to hear you praying
at any time of day.
Chorus:

2. In any place you go to
our Father God is there;
he knows what you are thinking,
he listens to each prayer.

131

Traditional

1. Someone's lonely, Lord, give him friends;
(*3 times*)
O Lord, give him friends.
Chorus:
Kum ba yah, my Lord, kum ba yah!
Kum ba yah, my Lord, kum ba yah!
Kum ba yah, my Lord, kum ba yah!
O Lord, kum ba yah!

2. Someone's fighting, Lord, give him peace;
O Lord, give him peace.
Chorus:

3. Someone's hating, Lord, give him love;
O Lord, give him love.
Chorus:

4. Someone's doubting, Lord, give him faith;
O Lord, give him faith.
Chorus:

5. We are living, Lord, help us care;
O Lord, help us care.
Chorus:

132

Diane Davis Andrew

1. Thank you, Lord, for this fine day, *(3 times)*
right where we are.

Chorus: *Alleluia, praise the Lord!*
Alleluia, praise the Lord!
Alleluia, praise the Lord,
right where we are.

2. Thank you, Lord, for loving us, *(3 times)*
right where we are.
Chorus:

3. Thank you, Lord, for giving us peace, *(3 times)*
right where we are.
Chorus:

4. Thank you, Lord, for setting us free, *(3 times)*
right where we are.
Chorus:

5. Thank you, Lord, for games to play, *(3 times)*
right where we are.
Chorus:

133

James E Seddon

1. Tell all the world of Jesus,
our Saviour, Lord and King;
and let the whole creation
of his salvation sing:
proclaim his glorious greatness
in nature and in grace;
creator and redeemer,
the Lord of time and space.

2. Tell all the world of Jesus,
that everyone may find
the joy of his forgiveness –
true peace of heart and mind:
proclaim his perfect goodness,
his deep, unfailing care,
his love so rich in mercy,
a love beyond compare.

3. Tell all the world of Jesus,
that everyone may know
of his almighty triumph
defeating every foe:
proclaim his coming glory,
when sin is overthrown,
and he shall reign in splendour –
the king upon his throne!

134

Alliene Vale

1. The joy of the Lord is my strength,
the joy of the Lord is my strength,
the joy of the Lord is my strength,
the joy of the Lord is my strength!

2. If you know the love of Jesus you will sing for
joy, *(3 times)*
the joy of the Lord is my strength!

135

From Psalm 23
Traditional

The Lord is my shepherd,
I'll follow him always.
He leads me by still waters,
I'll follow him always.
Always, always, I'll follow him always.
Always, always, I'll follow him always.

136

Traditional

Chorus:
Rise, and shine, and give God his glory, glory.
Rise, and shine, and give God his glory, glory.
Rise, and shine, and give God his glory, glory,
children of the Lord.

1. The Lord said to Noah: 'There's gonna be a
floody, floody.'
Lord said to Noah: 'There's gonna be a floody,
floody.
Get those children out of the muddy, muddy,
children of the Lord.'

Chorus:

2. The Lord told Noah to build him an arky, arky,
the Lord told Noah to build him an arky, arky.
Build it out of gopher barky, barky,
children of the Lord.

Chorus:

3. The animals, the animals, they came on, by
twosies, twosies,
the animals, the animals, they came on, by
twosies, twosies,
elephants and kangaroosies, 'roosies,
children of the Lord.

Chorus:

4. It rained and poured for forty daysies, daysies,
it rained and poured for forty daysies, daysies,
almost drove those animals crazyies, crazyies,
children of the Lord.

Chorus:

5. The sun came out and dried up the landy,
landy,
the sun came out and dried up the landy,
landy,
everything was fine and dandy, dandy,
children of the Lord.

Chorus:

137

Unknown

This is my commandment, that you love one another,
that your joy may be full.
This is my commandment, that you love one another,
that your joy may be full,
that your joy may be full,
that your joy may be full.
This is my commandment, that you love one another,
that your joy may be full.

Other verses may be added:

This is my commandment, that you
'trust one another . . .'
'serve one another . . .'

138

Charles High

This is the day of the Lord,
this is the day of the Lord,
this is the day of the Lord,
allelu, allelu!

Alternative verses:

This is the (feast . . . birthday . . . service . . . song) of the Lord.
We are the people of the Lord.
These are the praises of the Lord.

139

Unknown

1. This is the day, this is the day
that the Lord has made,
that the Lord has made;
we will rejoice, we will rejoice,
and be glad in it, and be glad in it.
This is the day that the Lord has made,
we will rejoice and be glad in it;
this is the day, this is the day
that the Lord has made.

2. This is the day, this is the day
when he rose again . . .

3. This is the day, this is the day
when the Spirit came . . .

140

James E Seddon

1. To him we come –
Jesus Christ our Lord,
God's own living Word,
his dear Son:
in him there is no east and west,
in him all nations shall be blessed;
to all he offers peace and rest –
  loving Lord!

2. In him we live –
Christ our strength and stay,
life and truth and way,
friend divine;

his power can break the chains of sin,
still all life's storms without, within,
help us the daily fight to win –
living Lord!

3. For him we go –
soldiers of the cross,
counting all things loss
him to know;
going to every land and race,
preaching to all redeeming grace,
building his church in every place –
conquering Lord!

4. With him we serve –
his the work we share
with saints everywhere,
near and far;
one in the task which faith requires,
one in the zeal which never tires,
one in the hope his love inspires –
coming Lord!

5. Onward we go –
faithful, bold and true,
called his will to do
day by day
till, at the last, with joy we'll see
Jesus, in glorious majesty;
live with him through eternity –
reigning Lord!

141

Gordon Carter

1. When I'm tired, when I'm sad, no one cares for me.
He was tired, he was sad, and he died for me.
He was tired, he was sad, and he died for me.

2. When I'm hurt, when I'm ill, feeling misery,
he is here, reaching near, giving sympathy.
(*repeat*)

3. When the pain and the shame are too much to bear,
Jesus stands, open hands, showing he is there.
(*repeat*)

4. On the hill, all alone, Jesus died for all.
When I'm tired, when I'm sad, I will hear him call. (*repeat*)

142

P M Verrall

1. Would you walk by on the other side,
when someone called for aid?
Would you walk by on the other side,
and would you be afraid?

Chorus:
Cross over the road my friend,
ask the Lord his strength to lend,
his compassion has no end,
cross over the road.

2. Would you walk by on the other side
when you saw a loved one stray?
Would you walk by on the other side,
or would you watch and pray?
Chorus:

3. Would you walk by on the other side,
when starving children cried?
Would you walk by on the other side,
and would you not provide?
Chorus: (repeat last line 3 times)

143

John Glandfield

1. When Jesus walked in Galilee,
he gave all men a chance to see
what God intended them to be;
and how they ought to live.

2. When Jesus hung upon the cross,
enduring hunger, pain and loss,
he looked with loving eyes across
the scene and said, 'Forgive.'

3. When Jesus rose on Easter Day,
he met a woman in the way,
and said, 'Go to my friends, and say
the Master is alive.'

4. When Jesus comes to us each day,
and listens to us as we pray,
we'll listen too and hear him say
'Come, follow me, and live.'

THE BIBLE

144

Brian Wren

1. Deep in the shadows of the past,
far out from settled lands,
some nomads travelled with their God
across the desert sands.
The dawn of hope for humankind
was glimpsed by them alone –
a promise calling them ahead,
a future yet unknown.

2. While others bowed to changeless gods
they met a mystery;
God with an uncompleted name,
'I am what I will be';
and by their tents, around their fires,
in story, song and law,
they praised, remembered, handed on
a past that promised more.

3. From Abraham to Nazareth
the promise changed and grew,
while some, remembering the past,
recorded what they knew,
and some, in letters or laments,
in prophecy and praise,
recovered, held and re-expressed
new hope for changing days.

4. For all the writings that survived,
for leaders, long ago,
who sifted, chose, and then preserved
the Bible that we know,
give thanks, and find its promise yet
our comfort, strength and call –
the working model for our faith
alive with hope for all.

145

Christopher Idle

1. Lord, you sometimes speak in wonders,
unmistakable and clear;
mighty signs to prove your presence,
overcoming doubt and fear.

2. Lord, you sometimes speak in whispers,
still and small and scarcely heard;
only those who want to listen
catch the all-important word.

3. Lord, you sometimes speak in silence,
through our loud and noisy day;
we can know and trust you better
when we quietly wait and pray.

4. Lord, you often speak in Scripture –
words that summon from the page,
shown and taught us by your Spirit
with fresh light for every age.

5. Lord, you always speak in Jesus,
always new yet still the same;
teach us now more of our Saviour;
make our lives display his name.

146

R T Brooks

1. Praise to God whose word was spoken
in the deed that made the earth.
His the voice that called a nation,
his the fires that tried her worth.
God has spoken, God has spoken:
praise him for his saving word.

2. Praise to God whose word was written
in the Scripture's sacred page,
record of the revelation
showing him to every age.
God has spoken, God has spoken:
praise him for his saving word.

3. Praise to God whose Word incarnate
glorified the flesh of man.
Deeds and words and death and rising
tell the grace in heaven's plan.
God has spoken, God has spoken:
praise him for his saving word.

4. Praise to God who through his Spirit
ever speaks his word to man.
Spirit, dwelling deep within us,
show us all the Father's plan.
God is speaking, God is speaking:
praise him for his saving word.

ALL GOD'S PEOPLE

147

Unknown

1. Come and go with me to my Father's house,
to my Father's house, to my Father's house;
come and go with me to my Father's house
where there's joy, joy, joy!

2. It's not very far to my Father's house,
to my Father's house, to my Father's house;
come and go with me to my Father's house
where there's joy, joy, joy!

3. There is room for all in my Father's house,
in my Father's house, in my Father's house;
come and go with me to my Father's house
where there's joy, joy, joy!

4. Everything is free in my Father's house,
in my Father's house, in my Father's house;
come and go with me to my Father's house
where there's joy, joy, joy!

5. Jesus is the way to my Father's house,
to my Father's house, to my Father's house;
come and go with me to my Father's house
where there's joy, joy, joy!

6. Jesus is the light in my Father's house,
in my Father's house, in my Father's house;
come and go with me to my Father's house
where there's joy, joy, joy!

148

James E Seddon

1. Go forth and tell! O church of God, awake!
God's saving news to all the nations take.
Proclaim Christ Jesus, Saviour, Lord and King,
that all the world his worthy praise may sing.

2. Go forth and tell! God's love embraces all;
he will in grace respond to all who call.
How shall they call if they have never heard
the gracious invitation of his word?

3. Go forth and tell! Men still in darkness lie:
in wealth or want, in sin they live and die.
Give us, O Lord, concern of heart and mind,
a love like thine which cares for all mankind.

4. Go forth and tell! The doors are open wide:
share God's good gifts with men so long denied.
Live out your life as Christ, your Lord, shall
choose,
your ransomed powers for his sole glory use.

5. Go forth and tell! O church of God, arise:
go in the strength which Christ your Lord
supplies.
Go, till all nations his great name adore
and serve him Lord and King for evermore.

149

Jimmy Owens

1. He is here, he is here,
he is moving among us;
he is here, he is here,
as we gather in his name!
He is here, he is here,
and he wants to work a wonder;
he is here
as we gather in his name.

2. He is Lord, he is Lord,
let us worship before him;
He is Lord, he is Lord,
as we gather in his name!
He is Lord, he is Lord,
let us praise and adore him –
yesterday and today
and for evermore the same.

150

Richard Avery and Donald Marsh

Chorus:
I am the church![1] *You are the church!*[2] *We are the church together!*[3]
All who follow Jesus.[4] *All around the world.*[5] *Yes we're the church together.*[6]

1. The church is not a building, the church is not a steeple.
The church is not a resting place, the church is a people!

2. We're many kinds of people with many kinds
 of faces;
all colours and all ages, too, from all times and
 places.

3. Sometimes the church is marching, sometimes
 it's bravely burning,
sometimes it's riding, sometimes hiding.
 Always it's learning!

4. And when the people gather there's singing
 and there's praying,
there's laughing and there's crying sometimes,
 all of it saying:

5. At Pentecost some people received the Holy
 Spirit
and told the good news through the world to all
 who would hear it.

6. I count if I am ninety, or nine, or just a baby;
there's one thing I am sure about and I don't
 mean maybe:

Actions:

1. With your thumb, point to yourself.
2. Point to your partner.
3. Shake hands.
4. Reach out with both hands.
5. Circle arms over head.
6. Link arms.

151

John Oxenham

1. In Christ there is no east or west,
in him no south or north,
but one great fellowship of love
throughout the whole wide earth.

2. Join hands, then, brothers of the faith,
whate'er your race may be;
who serves my Father as a son
is surely kin to me.

3. In Christ now meet both east and west,
in him meet south and north,
all Christly souls are one in him,
throughout the whole wide earth.

152

Carol Rose

1. The church is wherever God's people are
praising,
singing their thanks for the joy of this day.
The church is wherever disciples of Jesus
remember his story and walk in his way.

2. The church is wherever God's people are
helping,
caring for neighbours in sickness and need.
The church is wherever God's people are
sharing
the words of the Bible in gift and in deed.

153

The Grace
St Aidan's Community

May the grace of our Lord Jesus Christ
and the love of God our Father,
and the fellowship, the fellowship
of the Holy Spirit be with us
for evermore, and evermore, and evermore,
Amen.

154

Michael Lehr

Shalom, my friend,
God's peace, my friend,
go with you now;
and stay with you
in all you do.
Shalom! Shalom!

155

Andrae Crouch

1. Soon and very soon
we are going to see the King,
soon and very soon
we are going to see the King,
soon and very soon
we are going to see the King.
Alleluia, alleluia, we're going to see the King!

2. No more cryin' there
we are going to see the King,
no more cryin' there
we are going to see the King,
no more cryin' there
we are going to see the King.
Alleluia, alleluia, we're going to see the King!

3. No more dyin' there
we are going to see the King,
no more dyin' there
we are going to see the King,
no more dyin' there
we are going to see the King.
Alleluia, alleluia, we're going to see the King!
Alleluia, alleluia, alleluia, alleluia.

4. Soon and very soon
we are going to see the King,
soon and very soon
we are going to see the King,
soon and very soon
we are going to see the King.
Alleluia, alleluia, we're going to see the King!
Allcluia, alleluia, alleluia, alleluia.

156

Colin Sterne

1. We've a story to tell to the nations,
that shall turn their hearts to the right;
a story of truth and mercy,
a story of peace and light, a story of peace and light.

Chorus:
For the darkness shall turn to dawning,
and the dawning to noon-day bright,
and Christ's great kingdom shall come on earth,
the kingdom of love and light.

2. We've a song to be sung to the nations,
that shall lift their hearts to the Lord;
a song that shall conquer evil,
and shatter the spear and sword, and shatter
the spear and sword.

Chorus:

3. We've a message to give to the nations,
that the Lord who is reigning above,
has sent us his Son to save us,
and show us that God is love, and show us that
God is love.

Chorus:

4. We've a Saviour to show to the nations,
who the path of sorrow has trod,
that all of the world's great people
might come to the truth of God, might come to
the truth of God.

Chorus:

INDEX OF FIRST LINES